MY LIFE LIST

STERLING

New York
www.ster

STERLING and the distinctive Sterling logo are registered trademarks of
Sterling Publishing Co., Inc.

1   3   5   7   9   10   8   6   4   2

Published by Sterling Publishing Co., Inc.
387 Park Avenue South, New York, NY 10016
© 2009 by Sterling Publishing Co., Inc.
Distributed in Canada by Sterling Publishing
c/o Canadian Manda Group, 165 Dufferin Street
Toronto, Ontario, Canada M6K 3H6
Distributed in the United Kingdom by GMC Distribution Services
Castle Place, 166 High Street, Lewes, East Sussex, England BN7 1XU
Distributed in Australia by Capricorn Link (Australia) Pty. Ltd.
P.O. Box 704, Windsor, NSW 2756, Australia

Sterling ISBN 978-1-4027-6238-3

For information about custom editions, special sales, premium and
corporate purchases, please contact Sterling Special Sales
Department at 800-805-5489 or specialsales@sterlingpublishing.com.

Design by Fritz Metsch

THIS JOURNAL BELONGS TO:

_____

CREATING YOUR LIFE LIST

This book gives you the freedom to start an exciting journey. It gives you a place to think about and write down the things you want to accomplish in your life, the places you want to go, and the person you want to become. You have the right to revisit, rework, delete, and expand on your vision as you go along, from day to day and month to month. Your dreams—or whatever you hope to accomplish in life—are your most precious assets, but unless you make a conscious effort to explore your goals, you may never be able to fully achieve them. The process begins with making a life list, which sounds simple enough, but if you're not used to thinking in a strategic way about your goals—or about a time frame in which achieve them—it's helpful to have a few prompts, a plan, and a dollop of inspiration to stay motivated and on course. This book will show you how to do just that.

You Can Get There from Here

A life list is just like a road map that connects the dots between your goals and shows you

> *It's never too late to be who you might have been.*
>
> GEORGE ELIOT
>
> ❧

how to achieve them. In order to get there, you'll need to carve a little time out of your everyday schedule—a small gift to yourself that will pay off. It can take as little time as savoring a good cup of coffee or making a shopping list. In fact, research has actually shown that the simple exercise of recording a goal increases the likelihood that you will achieve it. As the old saying goes, "Goals that are not written down are just wishes."

Making a life list should be fun and doable, not a chore. The minute it begins to feel like homework, step back, relax, and do something else for a while. It's understandable why you might be reluctant to set new goals, especially if you have had trouble sticking to New Year's resolutions, but there is no right or wrong about goal setting. When you satisfy your goals in the areas of life that mean the most to you—your career, your family and friends, school, creative endeavors, health, your spiritual life, fitness, service to your community, or just sleeping better—you become happier.

The mission of this journal is to prove that you can have fun and enjoy the process of actually reaching your goals, as long as they are exactly that: *your* goals, not someone else's. If the goals on your list make you feel more hopeful and optimistic, so much the better. This optimism will flow into every area of your life and energize it from the top down. Your life list should be a refuge, a place you can sink into like a favorite easy chair and let your mind drift. Where *do* you want to go with your life?

> *Act as though what you do makes a difference. It does.*
>
> WILLIAM JAMES

Putting Your Dreams into Motion

Researchers in the area of learned optimism and applied positive psychology have been studying the principles of goal setting for decades to understand which goals provide the most satisfaction and to learn how to set solid, achievable targets. Studies and anecdotal evidence based on the experience of many thousands of people show that your life list goals will give you the most satisfaction if they are . . .

. . . concrete rather than abstract.

Vague goals (eat more healthy food, become a better person, lose a little weight) can slide away from you if they're not clearly defined. How much is "a little" weight? What exactly does it mean to become a "better" person? On the other hand, specific goals (eat two pieces of fruit every day, volunteer at a homeless shelter once a month, lose 5 pounds) give you a solid game plan. This doesn't mean that abstract goals aren't worthwhile. It's just that you may need to think a bit about how to transform them into concrete goals.

. . . intrinsic rather than extrinsic.

Psychologists who study the subject of quality of life issues tell us that most goals can be grouped into one of two categories: intrinsic goals, such as having good health, enjoying satisfying relationships, and contributing to the greater good of the community; and extrinsic goals, which include ambitions like having power over others, acquiring money or material goods, and projecting a successful image to friends or colleagues. Research has shown that setting and striving to reach *intrinsic* goals rather than extrinsic goals results in more happiness and better overall health and psychological well-being.

. . . measurable. If you don't track your progress, you won't know when or if you've been successful. "Spend more time with the kids" is a goal that cannot be measured in

any meaningful way. But "Play outside for three hours with the kids each Saturday morning" is. When you can measure your progress toward a goal, you know for sure when you've been successful, which is what goal setting is all about.

. . . challenging but attainable. When a target is too easy to reach, there's no joy or excitement in achieving it. On the other hand, if a goal is simply out of reach for you, no matter how hard you work for it or the sacrifices you make, failure and disappointment are inevitable, which is the exact opposite of how you want to feel about your ambitions. That's not to say you shouldn't dream big—on the contrary, that's what a life list and this journal are for. But if you find that you have been recording goals that you know are not possible or leave you disappointed, focus on what the feelings are behind those dreams. If your ultimate goal is to headline in a Broadway musical, but you have no dance or voice training, take some time to explore why you are drawn to it, instead of simply giving up. Is it the allure of being acknowledged publicly as a gifted, creative person? Is it the applause? The sheer joy of performance? Once you figure out the "goal behind the goal," you can almost always find a parallel dream that is equally fulfilling. As Maya Angelou has said, "Life loves to be taken by the lapel and told: I'm with you kid. Let's go."

. . . meaningful to you. It's no use recording a goal that your mother, partner, best friend, or mentor has always had for you. Of course you want the people you love and respect to be proud of you, but unless you truly want to do or be what they want for you, it is very unlikely to happen.

. . . tied to a specific deadline. The proposition "I want to take a windjammer cruise someday" is exciting and promising but it can't become a real goal on you life list unless you give yourself a deadline, a specific date. You need to fill in this dot on your road map to enjoy the most benefit from your goals. Assign a deadline to each item on your list. It can be a particular date or a time frame (next week, next month), but it must be specific.

Although simple goals may have a single deadline—"finish reading *War and Peace* by the end of December"—you'll want to break down more ambitious goals into smaller intermediate objectives. This serves two purposes: First, it makes the overall goal seem less daunting and second, reaching intermediate milestones gives your confidence a boost and allows you to enjoy successes on the way to achieving your ultimate goal.

Sarah, for example, is a young woman who wants to leave her current job as an administrative assistant to become a pediatric nurse. Although her goal is ambitious, it is completely achievable. But first Sarah needs to break it down into smaller intermediate steps such as:

- researching nursing schools to find the right program for her
- applying to nursing schools
- completing the financial aid applications

To see a further breakdown of the steps Sarah opted to take in order to achieve her goal, take a look at the chart on page 11.

> *Conditions are never just right. People who delay action until all factors are favorable do nothing.*
>
> WILLIAM FEATHER

How to Use This Journal

Now that you are more familiar with the basics of practical goal setting, grab a piece of paper and jot down the first four or five goals that pop into your head. The characters in the movie *The Bucket List* did just that, as have many other thousands of successful goal-seekers—it's the simplest, most direct way to change the direction of your life. If you like, head off to a quiet place like the beach, a park, your living room couch, or any other place where you feel calm and relaxed. There's no right or wrong way to create a life list, but if you're finding it difficult to focus on specific things that make you happy—the things you most desire—try playing a little trick on your mind and think about the first three things you would do if you suddenly won the lottery and were free to do anything you liked, without any limitations.

Or you might ask yourself what you would do if you had only one month to live. With whom would you spend that time? Where— and with whom—would you go, and what would you do, if your resources were unlimited and you looked and felt like a million dollars?

Think about someone you truly admire, whom you'd like to be, and focus on the qualities that make that person so great. What do the person's most admirable traits say about your own values? How do they translate into life goals for you?

And there's nothing wrong with asking a good friend or mentor what he or she would put on a life list. Their goals may give you some good ideas. You can also explore hundreds of Web sites on the Internet that are designed specifically for people to share their goals, post their struggles and triumphs, and cheer on others who are also striving to achieve their dreams. Here you can gather more ideas for your life list.

Now, take another look at the goals you've jotted down. What do your goals and values tell you about yourself and what you want? Are you surprised? Alarmed? Delighted? Composing a life list gives you the freedom to be completely honest about your ambitions and goals, whether it is to change your career or get out of a damaging relationship. You may want to travel, stop smoking, become a pastry chef, do volunteer work, start a company, learn to meditate, join an investment club, go back to school, spend more time with your family, or learn to knit. The possibilities are endless. All that matters is that the goals you choose are meaningful to you.

Once you have a list you're happy with (and remember, you're free to revise and change the terms of your list at any time), turn to the Goals List on page 15 and record your goals on the lines provided. Next, fill in the chart provided for each goal. You might want to use a pencil so that you can easily make changes. The main thing is to work at your own pace and enjoy the process. Recording and updating some of your goals may be easy and fast, light and fun, while others, such as the one in the chart on page 11, might require more serious consideration. As you will see, each goal chart provides space for you to record:

> *Don't limit yourself. Many people limit themselves to what they think they can do. You can go as far as your mind lets you. What you believe, you can achieve.*
>
> MARY KAY ASH

- What the goal is
- Why this goal is important to you
- Whether the goal is a short, intermediate, or long-term aspiration
- A targeted completion date

Next, you'll list the action steps needed to reach your goal. As you can see in the sample, the space allows you to break broader action steps into smaller ones. For instance, "research nursing schools" is a broad action step; "call local hospital administrative office," "visit library," "do online research," and "narrow down my list to three schools" are intermediate steps.

For each action item, record a projected completion date, and then check off each step as you finish it.

Several journal pages, where you can record your thoughts and feelings as you work toward your goal, follow each goal chart.

One of the most gratifying aspects of creating a life list is reaching your intermediate and long-term goals. Checking or crossing them off your list is a cause for celebration! Take the time to savor and share each of your achievements. Relish the sensation of feeling happy. Your newfound success with goal setting will make you a more optimistic person, with a stronger belief in your own effectiveness and powers. And, as an added benefit, you will be healthier, enjoy your life and friends more, and feel energized to be more successful in other areas of your life.

Handling Setbacks and Fine-tuning Your List

If you're not getting closer to one or more of your goals, but instead are feeling overwhelmed or are losing interest, don't be discouraged: Everything you've learned about being happy and working toward your goals will give you the energy to renew your efforts.

Pull out your list and read over the items that are giving you trouble, paying special attention to the meaning that you've assigned to them. Are these goals still important to you? Do they excite you in the same way that they did when you first recorded them?

JOHN GODDARD'S *ULTIMATE LIFE LIST*

Become an Eagle Scout

Dive in a submarine

Land on and take off from an aircraft carrier

Fly in a blimp, balloon, and glider

Ride an elephant, camel, ostrich, and bronco

Skin dive to forty feet and hold breath two and a half minutes underwater

Catch a ten-pound lobster and a ten-inch abalone

Play flute and violin

Type fifty words a minute

Make a parachute jump

TO MOST PEOPLE, *this may look like the life list of someone who is doomed to be chronically disappointed. But in fact, it represents just a few of the 111 goals already reached at this writing by John Goddard, a native Californian who composed his 127-item life list in 1940 when he was just fifteen years old. Among the other items on his list: Climb the Matterhorn, Mount Rainier, and Mount Fuji; visit the North and South poles; read the Bible from cover to cover; and become proficient in the use of a plane, motorcycle, tractor, surfboard, rifle, pistol, canoe, microscope, football, basketball, bow and arrow, lariat, and boomerang.*

During the last couple of decades, John has concentrated more on writing and motivational speaking than on having adventures, but he still serves as an inspiration to all of us who want to live our lives to the hilt.

Goal:	*Change career from administrative assistant to nurse.*
Why this goal is important to me:	*I want to help people and make more money*
Type of goal:	Short ☐ Intermediate ☐ Long-term ✓
Completion date:	*1/1/2011*

Action Steps	Projected completion date	Actual completion date
Research nursing schools		
Call local hospital administrative office	*3/8/09*	*3/8/09*
Visit library	*3/11/09*	*3/11/09*
Do online research	*4/15/09*	*4/15/09*
Narrow down my list to three schools	*6/15/09*	*7/1/09*
Apply to nursing schools	*12/1/09*	*12/1/09*
Ask friend who's a nurse for recommendation	*7/8/09*	*7/8/09*
Put money aside for application fees	*8/1/09*	*10/15/09*
Complete financial aid applications	*11/1/09*	*11/1/09*
Look into scholarships available from the schools I apply to	*7/8/09*	*7/29/09*
Complete student loan application	*9/1/09*	*9/1/09*
Make several copies of tax forms	*5/1/09*	*5/1/09*
Give notice at my job	*3/1/10*	*3/1/10*
Roll over 401(k) plan	*4/1/10*	*4/1/10*
Make sure husband puts me on his health insurance	*3/1/10*	*3/1/10*
Success!		✓
I revised or eliminated this goal		Yes ☐ No ☐
Why?		

If not, put them on the back burner for awhile and reconsider them later. You haven't failed if you decide to revise or eliminate a goal altogether. Recognizing that a dream is no longer important to you is a step forward; pursuing a goal that no longer has meaning is not.

If a particular goal continues to inspire you, but you can't seem to get any closer to it, perhaps the problem lies not in the goal itself, but in the plan you've set out to reach that goal. Are the intermediate milestones too daunting? Have you suddenly become too busy to meet your own deadlines? Maybe the answer is simply that you need to refocus or push yourself a bit more. Or maybe you're wondering if there are too few goals on your list and feel as if you're not accomplishing as much as you would like. On the other hand, too many goals may feel overwhelming. If the items on your list begin to feel like dreaded to-dos, the point is lost. Some days maybe harder than others, it's true, but there should always be an undercurrent feeling of "I want this" whenever you review your list.

Only you can determine the "correct" number of goals for your list, but you may want to start with a lower number first, until you have a handle on working with your life list and become accustomed to reviewing

> *There is the risk you cannot afford to take, and there is the risk you cannot afford not to take.*
>
> PETER DRUCKER

it and tracking your progress. This journal provides enough pages and charts for you to record 37 goals. Remember: Your lists can grow and change as you do. You are always free to add and modify a goal, or completely eliminate one—each goal chart includes a space for you to do just that.

Keeping Your Eye on the Prize

You may decide to share your list with friends or family—or even post it to a life list Web site. Some experts in goal setting suggest that sharing goals is a good way to maintain your accountability and keep you on the right track. Once again, this is up to you. You might enjoy the encouragement and kudos. On the other hand, you may feel put under the microscope and pressured to perform.

What are the next steps? Be diligent about checking your list—once a day may be too often, but once a week isn't unreasonable. You've taken time to plant these seeds and they'll need your care to sprout, grow, and bloom. You may face ups and downs. But over the long haul it's important to be flexible: Life will happen. And, surprisingly, roadblocks and setbacks can spark excellent revisions and additions.

21 Ways to Make Your Life List Happen

- Read inspiring novels, memoirs, and biographies of people who have fulfilled their ambitions and dreams.
- Make a list of people you admire and who have actually realized their dreams.
- Watch movies such as *The Bucket List* or *The Last Vacation* for inspiration and role models.
- Check out life lists and goal-setting sites on the Internet; it'll give you a stronger sense of community and connection with other people who are traveling the same road you are.
- Make your goals public by posting them on the Internet, on the door to your office or dorm room, or on the refrigerator, if it makes you feel more accountable and motivates you to achieve your goals.
- Surround yourself with positive imagery (photos of happy occasions, for example, or people who make you feel happy and accepted).
- Don't be afraid to take risks.
- Learn to focus better on your goals by taking a meditation or yoga class.

Energy and persistence conquer all things.

BENJAMIN FRANKLIN

You only live once—but if you work it right, once is enough.

JOE E. LEWIS

- Exercise and get the rest you need to feel energized.
- Stay attuned to the people around you—your family, friends, and peers—and make an effort to really listen to what they are saying.
- Renew you capacity to feel awe and a sense of peace by spending as much time as you can in nature.
- Don't be discouraged by setbacks; get support and feedback from a friend who is pursuing the same path you are, and get re-energized by other activities that make you feel competent, directed, and successful.
- Do what you can to reduce the amount of stress in your life through journal writing (or any other creative outlet that gives you pleasure and self-satisfaction). Sometimes a simple change of environment can make all the difference—especially if you walk there.
- Work at becoming more resilient and less rigid about your expectations; this will keep you from giving up entirely on certain goals.
- Accomplish as many small goals as you can; it'll give you confidence and a feeling of mastery when you go after bigger dreams.

- Stay positive and surround yourself with people whose outlook on life also is optimistic.
- Listen to music that inspires and keeps you focused on achieving your goals.
- Don't be afraid to revamp your life list from time to time; it's okay to get rid of old goals that are simply not that important to you anymore.
- Be adventurous about adding new goals to your list.
- Lighten up, slow down, and enjoy the ride.
- Celebrate your achievements, even the smallest victories; share them with others.

MY GOALS

Goal:

Why this goal is important to me:

Type of goal: love   Short ☐   Intermediate ☐   Long-term ☐

Completion date: 6/30/12

Action Steps	Projected completion date	Actual completion date
Success!		
I revised or eliminated this goal		Yes ☐ No ☐
Why?		

Nothing happens unless first a dream.

—CARL SANDBURG

Goal :

Why this goal is important to me :

Type of goal :　　　　　　Short ☐　　　Intermediate ☐　　　Long-term ☐

Completion date :

Action Steps	Projected completion date	Actual completion date

Success!

I revised or eliminated this goal　　　　　　Yes ☐　　No ☐

Why?

A jug fills drop by drop.

—BUDDHA

Goal :

Why this goal is important to me :

Type of goal :   Short ☐   Intermediate ☐   Long-term ☐

Completion date :

Action Steps	Projected completion date	Actual completion date

Success!

I revised or eliminated this goal		Yes ☐ No ☐
Why?		

Obstacles are those frightful things you see
when you take your eyes off your goals.

—SYDNEY SMITH

Goal:

Why this goal is important to me:

Type of goal: Short ☐   Intermediate ☐   Long-term ☐

Completion date:

Action Steps	Projected completion date	Actual completion date

Success!

I revised or eliminated this goal	Yes ☐ No ☐
Why?	

An aim in life is the only fortune worth the finding;
and it is not to be found in foreign lands, but in the heart itself.

—ROBERT LOUIS STEVENSON

Goal :

Why this goal is important to me :

Type of goal :   Short ☐   Intermediate ☐   Long-term ☐

Completion date :

Action Steps	Projected completion date	Actual completion date

Success!

I revised or eliminated this goal   Yes ☐   No ☐

Why?

Nobody is bored when he is trying to make something that is beautiful,
or to discover something that is true.

—WILLIAM INGE

Goal :

Why this goal is important to me :

| Type of goal : | Short ☐ | Intermediate ☐ | Long-term ☐ |

Completion date :

Action Steps	Projected completion date	Actual completion date

Success!

| I revised or eliminated this goal | Yes ☐   No ☐ |

Why?

Life loves to be taken by the lapel and told:
I'm with you, kid. Let's go.

—MAYA ANGELOU

Goal :

Why this goal is important to me :

| Type of goal : | Short ☐ | Intermediate ☐ | Long-term ☐ |

Completion date :

Action Steps	Projected completion date	Actual completion date

Success!

| I revised or eliminated this goal | Yes ☐   No ☐ |

Why?

True happiness comes from the joy of deeds well done,
the zest of creating things new.

—ANTOINE DE SAINT-EXUPÉRY

Goal :

Why this goal is important to me :

| Type of goal : | Short ☐ | Intermediate ☐ | Long-term ☐ |

Completion date :

Action Steps	Projected completion date	Actual completion date

Success!		
I revised or eliminated this goal	Yes ☐	No ☐
Why?		

Follow your own star!

—DANTE ALIGHIERI

Goal :

Why this goal is important to me :

Type of goal :   Short ☐   Intermediate ☐   Long-term ☐

Completion date :

Action Steps	Projected completion date	Actual completion date

Success!

I revised or eliminated this goal   Yes ☐   No ☐

Why?

If you have built castles in the air, your work need not be lost;
that is where they should be. Now put foundations under them.

—HENRY DAVID THOREAU

Goal :

Why this goal is important to me :

Type of goal :   Short ☐   Intermediate ☐   Long-term ☐

Completion date :

Action Steps	Projected completion date	Actual completion date

Success!

I revised or eliminated this goal	Yes ☐ No ☐

Why?

When you're finished changing, you're finished.

—BENJAMIN FRANKLIN

Goal :

Why this goal is important to me :

Type of goal :	Short	Intermediate	Long-term

Completion date :

Action Steps	Projected completion date	Actual completion date

Success!

I revised or eliminated this goal	Yes	No

Why?

Dreams come true. Without that possibility,
nature would not incite us to have them.

—JOHN UPDIKE

Goal :

Why this goal is important to me :

Type of goal :   Short ☐   Intermediate ☐   Long-term ☐

Completion date :

Action Steps	Projected completion date	Actual completion date

Success!

I revised or eliminated this goal	Yes ☐ No ☐
Why?	

Life is a promise; fulfill it.

—MOTHER THERESA

Goal :

Why this goal is important to me :

Type of goal : Short ☐ Intermediate ☐ Long-term ☐

Completion date :

Action Steps	Projected completion date	Actual completion date

Success!

I revised or eliminated this goal   Yes ☐   No ☐

Why?

The future belongs to those who believe in the beauty of their dreams.

—ELEANOR ROOSEVELT

Goal :

Why this goal is important to me :

| Type of goal : | Short ☐ | Intermediate ☐ | Long-term ☐ |

Completion date :

Action Steps	Projected completion date	Actual completion date

Success!

| I revised or eliminated this goal | Yes ☐ No ☐ |

Why?

Adventure is worthwhile.

—AMELIA EARHART

Goal :			
Why this goal is important to me :			
Type of goal :	Short ☐	Intermediate ☐	Long-term ☐
Completion date :			

Action Steps	Projected completion date	Actual completion date

Success!

I revised or eliminated this goal	Yes ☐ No ☐
Why?	

The thing always happens that you really believe in;
and the belief in a thing makes it happen.

—FRANK LLOYD WRIGHT

Goal :

Why this goal is important to me :

Type of goal :   Short ☐   Intermediate ☐   Long-term ☐

Completion date :

Action Steps	Projected completion date	Actual completion date

Success!

I revised or eliminated this goal   Yes ☐   No ☐

Why?

Life is ours to be spent, not to be saved.

—D. H. LAWRENCE

Goal :

Why this goal is important to me :

Type of goal : Short ☐   Intermediate ☐   Long-term ☐

Completion date :

Action Steps	Projected completion date	Actual completion date

Success!

I revised or eliminated this goal   Yes ☐   No ☐

Why?

Nobody gets to live life backward.
Look ahead, that is where your future lies.

—ANN LANDERS

Goal :			
Why this goal is important to me :			
Type of goal :	Short ☐	Intermediate ☐	Long-term ☐
Completion date :			

Action Steps	Projected completion date	Actual completion date

Success!

I revised or eliminated this goal	Yes ☐ No ☐
Why?	

Follow your bliss.

—JOSEPH CAMPBELL

Goal :			
Why this goal is important to me :			
Type of goal :	Short ☐	Intermediate ☐	Long-term ☐
Completion date :			

Action Steps	Projected completion date	Actual completion date

Success!		
I revised or eliminated this goal		Yes ☐ No ☐
Why?		

We all live in suspense from day to day;
in other words, you are the hero of your own story.

—MARY MCCARTHY

Goal :

Why this goal is important to me :

Type of goal :   Short ☐   Intermediate ☐   Long-term ☐

Completion date :

Action Steps	Projected completion date	Actual completion date

Success!

I revised or eliminated this goal   Yes ☐   No ☐

Why?

The desire accomplished is sweet to the soul.

—PROVERBS 13:19

Goal :

Why this goal is important to me :				
Type of goal :	Short ☐	Intermediate ☐	Long-term ☐	
Completion date :				

Action Steps	Projected completion date	Actual completion date

Success!

I revised or eliminated this goal	Yes ☐ No ☐	
Why?		

Success consists of getting up just one more time than you fall.

—OLIVER GOLDSMITH

Goal :

Why this goal is important to me :

Type of goal :   Short ☐   Intermediate ☐   Long-term ☐

Completion date :

Action Steps	Projected completion date	Actual completion date

Success!

I revised or eliminated this goal	Yes ☐ No ☐
Why?	

It is not enough to be busy. So are the ants.
The question is: What are we busy about?

—HENRY DAVID THOREAU

Goal :

Why this goal is important to me :

Type of goal : Short ☐ Intermediate ☐ Long-term ☐

Completion date :

Action Steps	Projected completion date	Actual completion date

Success!

I revised or eliminated this goal   Yes ☐   No ☐

Why?

Dance like no one is watching, Love like you'll never be hurt,
Sing like no one is listening, Live like it's heaven on earth.

—WILLIAM PURKEY

Goal :

Why this goal is important to me :

| Type of goal : | Short ☐ | Intermediate ☐ | Long-term ☐ |

Completion date :

Action Steps	Projected completion date	Actual completion date

Success!

| I revised or eliminated this goal | Yes ☐ No ☐ |

Why?

When I dream, I am ageless.

—ELIZABETH COATSWORTH

Goal :

Why this goal is important to me :

| Type of goal : | Short ☐ | Intermediate ☐ | Long-term ☐ |

Completion date :

Action Steps	Projected completion date	Actual completion date

Success!

| I revised or eliminated this goal | Yes ☐   No ☐ |
| Why? | |

Start by doing what's necessary, then what's possible,
and suddenly you are doing the impossible.

—FRANCIS OF ASSISI

Goal :			
Why this goal is important to me :			
Type of goal :	Short ☐	Intermediate ☐	Long-term ☐
Completion date :			

Action Steps	Projected completion date	Actual completion date

Success!		
I revised or eliminated this goal	Yes ☐	No ☐
Why?		

If we did the things we are capable of,
we would astound ourselves.

—THOMAS EDISON

Goal :			
Why this goal is important to me :			
Type of goal :	Short ☐	Intermediate ☐	Long-term ☐
Completion date :			

Action Steps	Projected completion date	Actual completion date

Success!	
I revised or eliminated this goal	Yes ☐ No ☐
Why?	

If you want to make good use of your time,
you've got to know what's most important and then give it all you've got.

—LEE IACOCCA

Goal :		
Why this goal is important to me :		
Type of goal :	Short ☐ Intermediate ☐	Long-term ☐
Completion date :		

Action Steps	Projected completion date	Actual completion date
Success!		
I revised or eliminated this goal		Yes ☐ No ☐
Why?		

Always dream and shoot higher than you know how to. Don't bother just to be better than your contemporaries or predecessors. Try to be better than yourself.

—WILLIAM FAULKNER

Goal:

Why this goal is important to me:

Type of goal: Short ☐ Intermediate ☐ Long-term ☐

Completion date:

Action Steps	Projected completion date	Actual completion date

Success!

I revised or eliminated this goal Yes ☐ No ☐

Why?

If you don't have a dream,
how you gonna have a dream come true?

—OSCAR HAMMERSTEIN II

Goal :

Why this goal is important to me :

Type of goal : Short ☐ Intermediate ☐ Long-term ☐

Completion date :

Action Steps	Projected completion date	Actual completion date

Success!

I revised or eliminated this goal	Yes ☐ No ☐

Why?

It is not death that a man should fear,
but he should fear never beginning to live.

— MARCUS AURELIUS

Goal :

Why this goal is important to me :

Type of goal :	Short	Intermediate	Long-term

Completion date :

Action Steps	Projected completion date	Actual completion date

Success!

I revised or eliminated this goal	Yes	No

Why?

The person who removes a mountain begins
by carrying away small stones.

—ANONYMOUS

Goal :

Why this goal is important to me :

Type of goal : Short ☐ Intermediate ☐ Long-term ☐

Completion date :

Action Steps	Projected completion date	Actual completion date

Success!

I revised or eliminated this goal Yes ☐ No ☐

Why?

Whatever fortune brings,
don't be afraid of doing things.

—A. A. MILNE

Goal :		
Why this goal is important to me :		
Type of goal :	Short ☐ Intermediate ☐	Long-term ☐
Completion date :		

Action Steps	Projected completion date	Actual completion date
Success!		
I revised or eliminated this goal	Yes ☐	No ☐
Why?		

Always bear in mind that your own resolution to succeed is more important than any one thing.

—ABRAHAM LINCOLN

Goal :

Why this goal is important to me :

Type of goal :   Short ☐   Intermediate ☐   Long-term ☐

Completion date :

Action Steps	Projected completion date	Actual completion date

Success!

I revised or eliminated this goal   Yes ☐   No ☐

Why?

Everything you want is out there waiting for you to ask.
Everything you want also wants you. But you have to take action to get it.

—JACK CANFIELD

Goal :

Why this goal is important to me :

| Type of goal : | Short ☐ | Intermediate ☐ | Long-term ☐ |

Completion date :

Action Steps	Projected completion date	Actual completion date

Success!

I revised or eliminated this goal	Yes ☐ No ☐
Why?	

It's time to start living the life you've imagined.

—HENRY JAMES

Goal:

Why this goal is important to me:

Type of goal: Short ☐   Intermediate ☐   Long-term ☐

Completion date:

Action Steps	Projected completion date	Actual completion date
Success!		
I revised or eliminated this goal	Yes ☐	No ☐
Why?		

Don't limit yourself. Many people limit themselves to what they think they can do.
You can go as far as your mind lets you. What you believe, you can achieve.

—MARY KAY ASH